Going up up up!

ISBN 0 7117 3728 2
Designed and produced by Jarrold Publishing
Text by Peter Rogers
Pictures: Action Images and Roger Harris
Project Manager: Malcolm Crampton
Design: Kaarin Wall
Reprographics: Martin Kempson
Editor: Sonya Calton
Printed in Great Britain. Jarrold Publishing 1/04
www.jarrold-publishing.co.uk

JARROLD
publishing

Going up up up!

By Peter Rogers

Norwich City
Football Club

Foreword

The 2003–04 season was a fantastic one for everyone connected with Norwich City Football Club and one we are all rightly proud of.

After winning promotion and then going on to land the First Division title, we enjoyed a wonderful few weeks at the end of last season. Although those final matches away to Watford and Sunderland and then at home to Preston will live long in the memory – I can honestly say I enjoyed the entire season.

From start to finish we faced many challenges and had to deal with a number of twists and turns along the way. This pictorial review of the campaign charts our progress throughout the season – from the start of pre-season training through to the never-to-be-forgotten Civic Reception at City Hall in May.

I'm sure all of our supporters will enjoy flicking though the pages of this publication as each picture represents a step along the way to our promotion dream.

Of course we all have our own favourite moment and most memorable match; therefore this book will serve as the perfect souvenir of the entire campaign and enable you to enjoy the 2003–04 season again and again in the months and years ahead.

Nigel Worthington

Introduction

There have been many great seasons that have shaped the Canaries' history. And without doubt the 2003–04 Nationwide First Championship-winning campaign will be remembered with great affection in the years to come.

Just like the famous '58–'59 cup run, promotion in '71–'72, the Milk Cup, Europe, and Cardiff – the 2003–04 season is sure to be added to the list of Norwich City's greatest ever campaigns.

It was the season that had it all – a comfortable double over arch-rivals Ipswich Town, the arrival of star striker Darren Huckerby, an England call for 'keeper Robert Green plus a hat-trick of Manager of the Month awards for boss Nigel Worthington. All finished off by a wonderful Civic Reception at City Hall in May.

The pages that follow in this pictorial review will enable fans to recall the Canaries' return to the big-time on a match-by-match basis. Whether it be the Leon McKenzie double at Portman Road, the Boxing Day signing of Darren Huckerby, the opening of the Jarrold Stand, the party at Watford or Iwan's farewell at Crewe – the images in this publication are sure to bring some great memories flooding back.

'On the ball City!'

Peter Rogers
July 2004

Contents

01|07|03

SIGNS
JIM BRENNAN

New signing Jim Brennan arrives at Colney prior to the start of pre-season training.

Canadian international Jim Brennan is introduced to the media at the Club's Colney Training Centre after becoming the Canaries' first summer signing ahead of the new campaign. With the ability to operate at either left-back or on the left-side of midfield, Jim joined from First Division rivals Nottingham Forest on a free transfer after being out of contract at the City Ground.

15|07|03

Pre-season friendly
Harwich & Parkeston 0
Norwich City 4

City played the first game of their pre-season schedule away to Harwich & Parkeston. A Canary side made up of both professionals and academy scholars ran out 4–0 winners with goals from Adam Smith, Olly Willis, Zema Abbey and Danny Crow.

16|07|03
Club photocall

At a sun-drenched Carrow Road the first team squad gather for the Club's annual photocall. The squad faces the camera modelling the latest kit with new Club sponsors Proton Cars and Lotus Cars logos on the shirts. Nigel Worthington and his staff are joined by only 21 players as the search for new players ahead of the big kick-off continues.

18|07|03

Pre-season training

The squad are put through their paces at Colney as pre-season training is stepped up-a-gear.

CLOCKWISE FROM RIGHT
Boss Nigel Worthington looks on; sit-ups in the sun; striker Zema Abbey takes a touch during this passing session; Paul McVeigh sprays the ball forward in a practice match

Club Captain Iwan Roberts leads the way as another lap of the training ground beckons

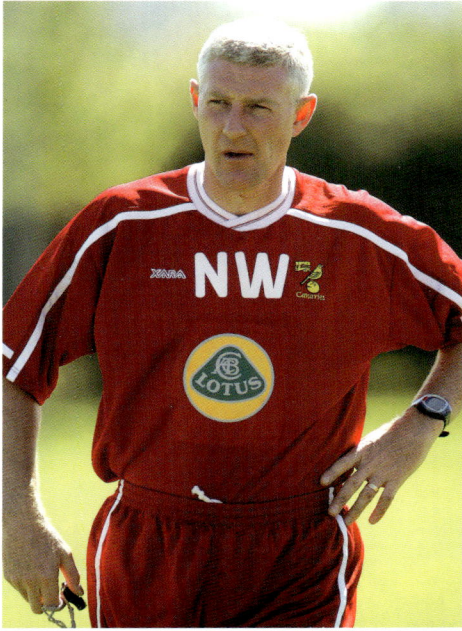

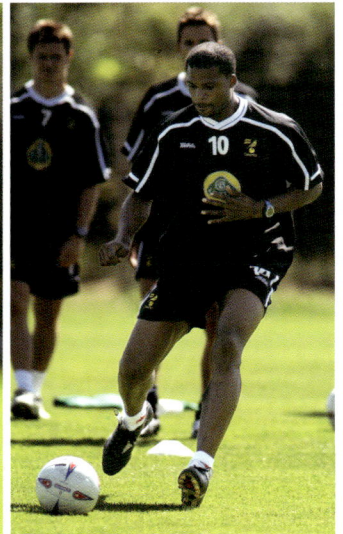

19|07|03

Pre-season friendly
Peterborough 0
Norwich City 0

Former Peterborough United defender Adam Drury enjoyed a successful return to London Road as he and his back four kept a clean sheet in a goalless friendly with the Second Division side.

22|07|03

SIGNS
DAMIEN FRANCIS

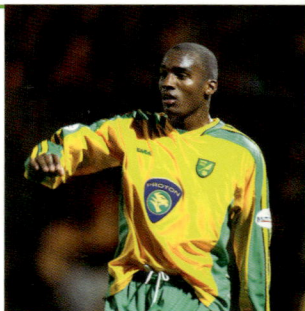

Boss Nigel Worthington makes his second signing of the summer with attacking midfielder Damien Francis arriving from cash-strapped Wimbledon. London born, Damien progressed through the ranks at Wimbledon to become one of the most highly-rated midfielders in the First Division.

22|07|03

Pre-season friendly
Norwich City 0
Spurs 3

Big spending Spurs arrive at Carrow Road with £6.25million Portuguese wonder-kid Helder Postiga in their line-up. Glenn Hoddle's side proves too much for City and run out comfortable 3–0 winners. The match marks the debut of Damien Francis and is Adam Drury's first match as Team Captain.

14

02|08|03

Pre-season friendly
Norwich City 2
FC Utrecht 0

With City's first game of the season away to Bradford just seven days away, Nigel Worthington's side play their final warm-up game as FC Utrecht visit Carrow Road. A second-half brace from Mark Rivers hands the Canaries a 2–0 win at Carrow Road.

06|08|03

LEAVES
DAREL RUSSELL

After months of uncertainty surrounding his future, midfielder Darel Russell moves on to fellow First Division side, Stoke City. The deal could net the Canaries up to £125,000.

08|08|03

SIGNS
MARC EDWORTHY

After arriving at Colney on trial only 24 hours earlier, experienced right-back Marc Edworthy puts pen-to-paper on a two-year contract with the Canaries and goes straight into the travelling party for the curtain raiser at Bradford the following day.

09|08|03

	P	GD	PTS
4 Millwall	1	2	3
5 Nottingham Forest	1	2	3
6 Crystal Palace	1	1	3
7 West Ham Utd	1	1	3
8 Bradford City	1	0	1
9 Norwich City	1	0	1

Bradford City 2
Norwich City 2

GOALS
Rivers
Easton
ATTENDANCE
13,159

City start the season in subtropical temperatures at Bradford's Valley Parade. A Mark Rivers penalty, followed by a Clint Easton strike looked to have set City on their way to victory but two late goals handed the Bantams a share of the spoils.

Malky Mackay goes head-to-head with Rotherham's Richie Barker

14|08|03

ON LOAN

ELVIS HAMMOND

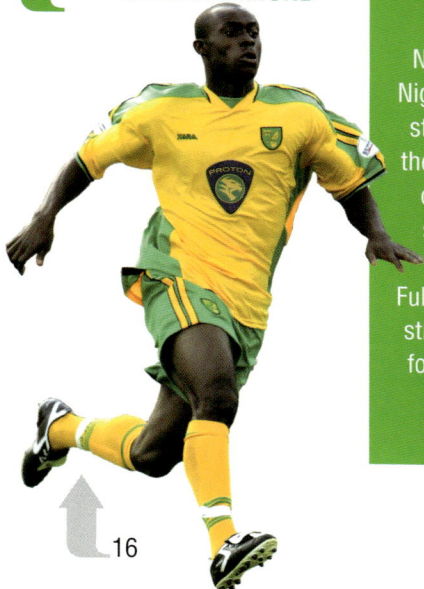

Following the disappointment of the League Cup exit at Northampton Town, boss Nigel Worthington moved to strengthen his squad with the one-month loan signing of Fulham's 22-year-old striker Elvis Hammond. A product of the Fulham Academy, Elvis went straight into the City squad for the first home game of the season against Rotherham United.

	P	GD	PTS
2 Millwall	2	3	6
3 Crystal Palace	2	2	6
4 Reading	2	3	4
5 Walsall	2	3	4
6 Bradford City	2	2	4
7 Norwich City	2	2	4

Norwich City 2
Rotherham Utd 0

GOALS

Rivers

Easton

ATTENDANCE

16,263

First-half goals from Mark Rivers and Clint Easton prove enough to give City a winning start to their Carrow Road campaign. Normally a tough nut to crack, Rotherham offer little as an attacking force and clearly miss the recently departed Alan Lee.

BELOW **Man of the Match Damien Francis sees his effort turned away by Rotherham 'keeper Mike Pollitt**

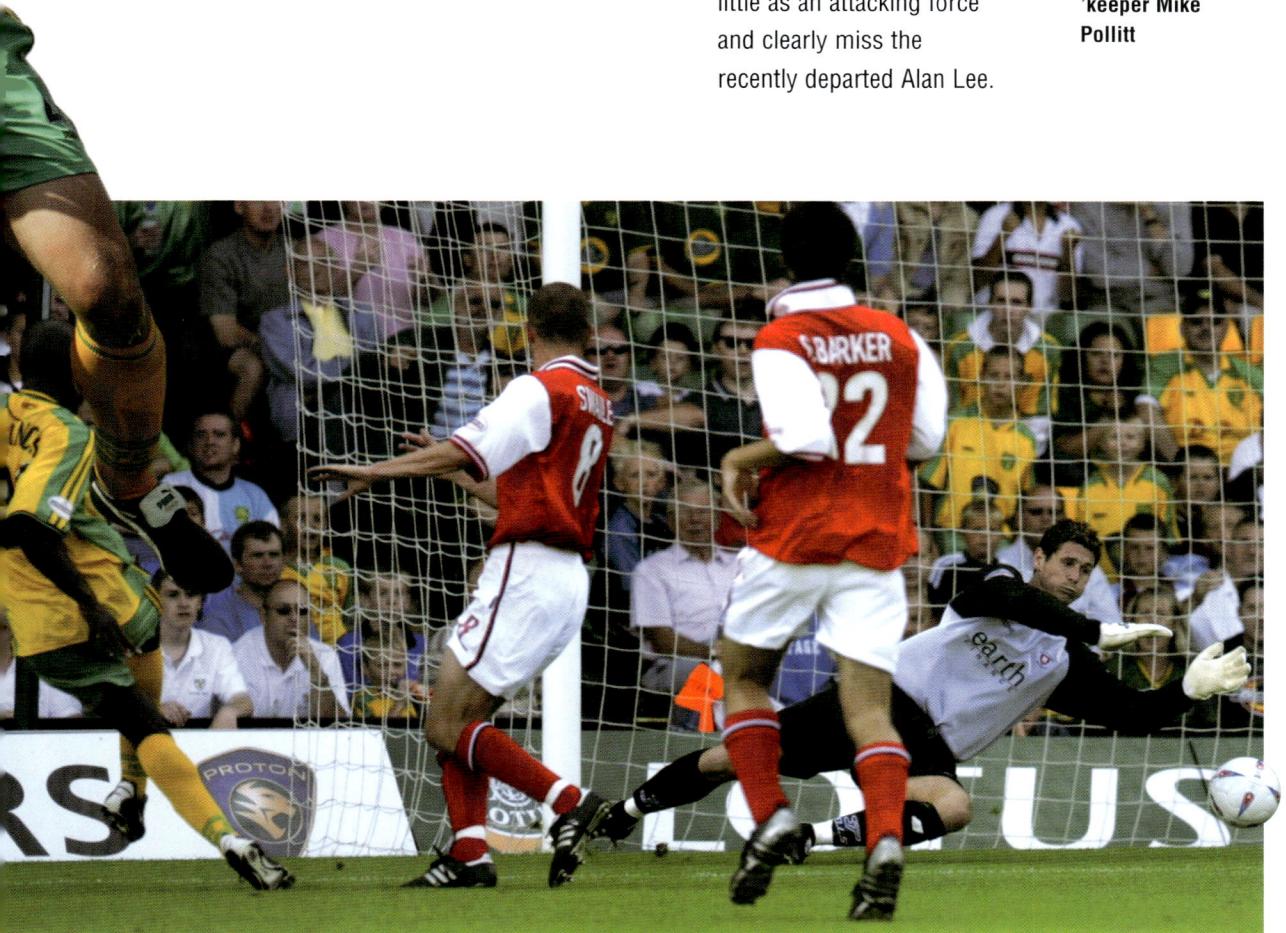

21|08|03

LEAVES

DAVID NIELSEN

Striker David Nielsen is granted a free-transfer back to Denmark after his wife is offered a new employment opportunity back in the couple's home country.

23|08|03

	P	GD	PTS
5 West Brom	3	1	6
6 Walsall	3	3	5
7 Gillingham	3	1	5
8 Sheffield Utd	3	1	5
9 Bradford City	3	1	4
10 Norwich City	3	1	4

Sheffield Utd 1
Norwich City 0

ATTENDANCE

24,285

Despite the backing of over 2,000 travelling fans, City fail to find top gear and slip to a disappointing 1–0 defeat. The match also sees striker Zema Abbey withdrawn with a knee injury.

18

26|08|03

	P	GD	PTS
2 West Brom	4	2	9
3 Reading	4	4	8
4 Stoke City	4	4	8
5 Millwall	4	3	8
6 Sheffield Utd	4	2	8
7 Norwich City	4	2	7

Norwich City 3 Wimbledon 2

GOALS

Francis

Rivers (2)

ATTENDANCE

16,082

Although the Canaries are struggling to make things happen on their travels, their home form remains very much intact. Nigel Worthington's side romp into a three-goal lead against the Dons with Damien Francis on target against his former employers. Wimbledon muster a level of respectability to the scoreline with two injury-time goals but the final score fails to reflect the Canaries' dominance.

28|08|03

INJURY

ZEMA ABBEY

The win over Wimbledon is soured by news of the injury sustained by Zema Abbey at Sheffield United. A cruciate anterior ligament injury in the left knee will rule Zema out for the remainder of the campaign.

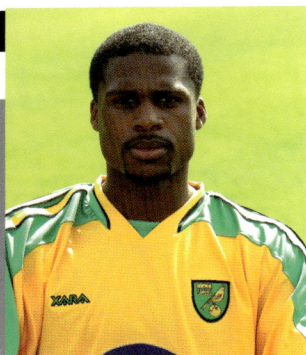

30|08|03

Nottm Forest 2
Norwich City 0

ATTENDANCE
21,058

Yet again City suffer travel sickness. A freak goal from David Johnson following a rare error from Robert Green hands Forest the advantage.
The hosts doubled their lead in the second half with a controversial penalty. Elvis Hammond went close for City whose miserable day was compounded by injuries to Iwan Roberts and Mark Rivers.

08|09|03

ON LOAN

CROUCH AND HUCKERBY

With injuries mounting and goals proving hard to come by – boss Nigel Worthington brings two Premiership strikers to Carrow Road on three-month loan deals. Aston Villa's giant frontman Peter Crouch and Manchester City's jet-heeled striker Darren Huckerby are unveiled at a Colney press conference and both players look set to start against Burnley, the Canaries' next game.

12|09|03

ON LOAN

KEVIN HARPER

Portsmouth's Kevin Harper becomes the Canaries' fourth loan signing of the season. The pacy midfielder joins Crouch and Huckerby in contention for a City debut the following day.

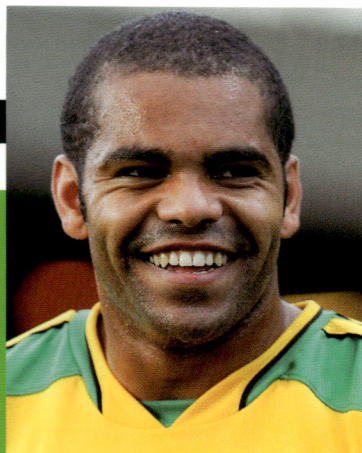

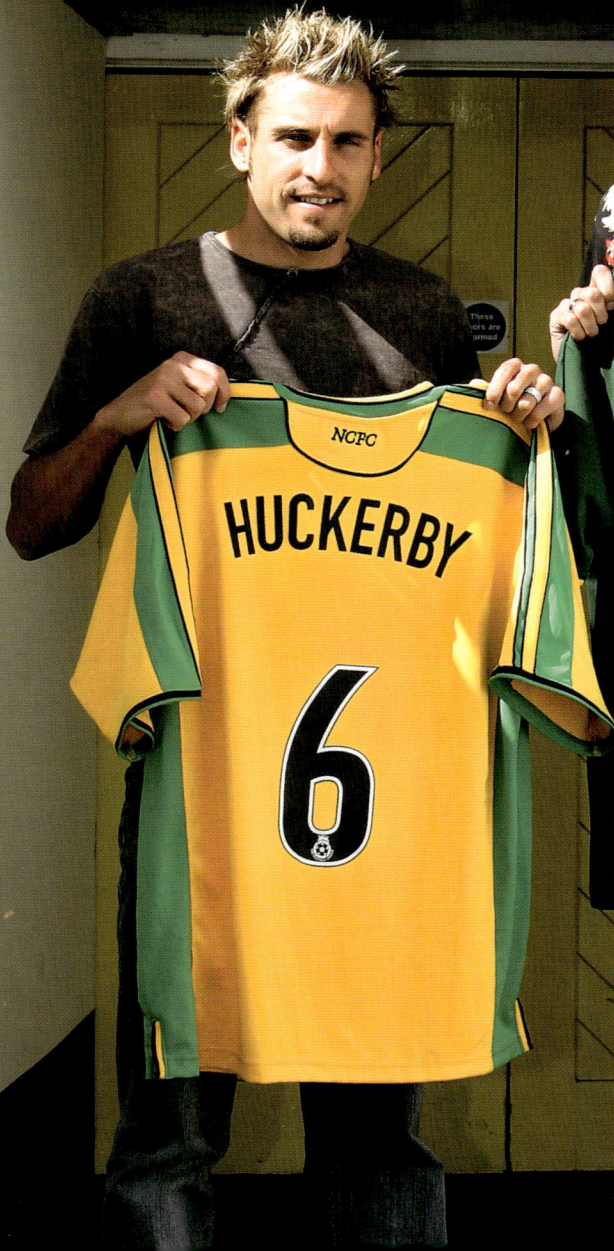

13|09|03

	P	GD	PTS
5 Nottingham Forest	6	4	12
6 Cardiff City	6	7	11
7 Reading	6	6	11
8 Sheffield Utd	6	1	11
9 Crystal Palace	6	2	10
10 Norwich City	6	2	10

Norwich City 2
Burnley 0

GOALS

Crouch

Roberts

ATTENDANCE

16,407

The three recent loan signings do the trick as a new-look Norwich side containing Crouch, Huckerby and Harper inspire the Canaries to a 2–0 win over Burnley. Crouch marks his debut with the first goal and Huckerby lays on a last-minute goal for substitute Iwan Roberts.

LEFT **Peter Crouch is mobbed after opening the scoring**
ABOVE **Darren Huckerby sprints away to set up Iwan Roberts**
FAR LEFT **Paul McVeigh fires in a shot**

16|09|03

		P	GD	PTS
2	West Ham Utd	7	6	16
3	Nottingham Forest	7	7	15
4	West Brom	7	5	15
5	Reading	7	7	14
6	Sheffield Utd	7	6	14
7	**Norwich City**	**7**	**3**	**13**

Gillingham 1
Norwich City 2

GOALS

Francis

Crouch

ATTENDANCE

8,022

The away day hoodoo comes to an end as goals from Peter Crouch and Damien Francis ensure City return to Carrow Road with maximum points from a difficult trip to Gillingham.

20|09|03

		P	GD	PTS
3	West Brom	8	5	16
4	West Ham Utd	8	4	16
5	Nottingham Forest	8	5	15
6	Millwall	8	3	15
7	Reading	8	6	14
8	**Norwich City**	**8**	**3**	**14**

Stoke City 1
Norwich City 1

GOALS

Huckerby

ATTENDANCE

10,672

In front of the Sky cameras the Canaries pick up a valuable point from a Saturday evening match at Stoke. Norwich trail 1–0 at the break but Darren Huckerby opens his goalscoring account with a fully-deserved second-half equaliser.

27|09|03

Norwich City 2
Crystal Palace 1

GOALS

Huckerby

Mackay

ATTENDANCE

16,425

The Canaries record their fourth straight home win of the season but had to come from behind to defeat a spirited Crystal Palace. City go one down in the opening minute but find a way back into the contest as Darren Huckerby converts a first-half penalty. A well-contested second period failed to separate the teams until Malky Mackay popped up with a late headed goal to the delight of the Carrow Road faithful.

30|09|03

Norwich City 2
Reading 1

GOALS

Huckerby
McVeigh

ATTENDANCE

16,387

City cap off September with yet another home win – this time it's the turn of Reading to leave Carrow Road empty-handed. City took the lead through Darren Huckerby, however the managerless Royals drew level prior to the break with a Nicky Forster goal. In similar fashion to the Palace game, City save their best to last and Paul McVeigh fires home a last-minute winner as Carrow Road erupts on 90 minutes for the second time in four days.

ABOVE LEFT **Paul McVeigh cracks home the Canaries' late winner**

02|10|03

LOAN EXTENDED

KEVIN HARPER

The impressive form of midfielder Kevin Harper sees the Portsmouth man agree to extend his loan spell at Carrow Road for a further two months.

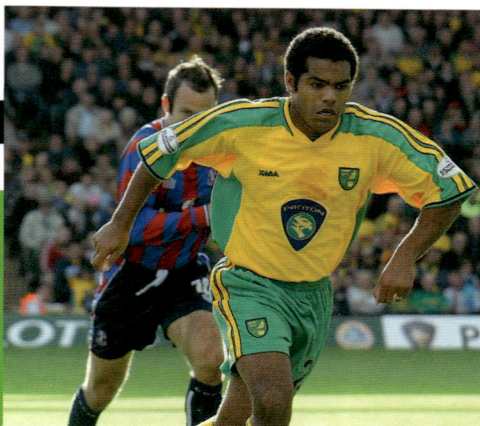

26

The Irish international expresses his delight as City make it five wins out of five at fortress Carrow Road

04|10|03

	P	GD	PTS
1 West Brom	11	9	25
2 Sheffield Utd	11	9	23
3 West Ham Utd	11	8	23
4 Sunderland	11	8	22
5 Wigan Athletic	11	8	22
6 Norwich City	11	5	21

Wigan Athletic 1 Norwich City 1

GOALS
Roberts
ATTENDANCE
9,346

City make a first visit to the JJB Stadium – the new home of high-flying Wigan Athletic. A wonder save from Robert Green to deny Geoff Horsfield and a second-half strike from Iwan Roberts ensure City return south with a useful point for their efforts.

10|10|03

Manager of the Month award

The Canaries' success in September saw boss Nigel Worthington win the Manager of the Month award. Nigel was presented with the award at Carrow Road after his side collected 13 points from a possible 15 in September.

15|10|03

West Ham Utd 1
Norwich City 1

GOALS
Crouch
ATTENDANCE
31,308

RIGHT **Trevor Brooking was unable to inspire West Ham to victory over City at Upton Park**

A trip to Upton Park for a meeting with title favourites West Ham United was next on the agenda for City. Under the guidance of caretaker manager Trevor Brooking, the Hammers took an early lead when Marc Edworthy deflected a cross past Robert Green for an unfortunate own-goal. The Canaries staged a spirited comeback and drew level with a Peter Crouch header in the second half. Damien Francis then hit the woodwork as City went in search of the winner.

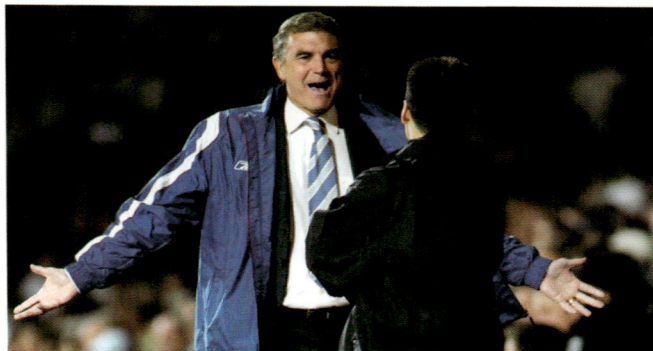

18|10|03

	P	GD	PTS
3 Sheffield Utd	13	9	26
4 Sunderland	13	9	26
5 West Ham Utd	13	8	25
6 Ipswich Town	14	6	23
7 Millwall	15	4	23
8 Norwich City	13	4	22

West Brom 1
Norwich City 0
ATTENDANCE
24,996

City faced their third away game on the spin with a trip to The Hawthorns. Despite a performance that warranted a point, City left empty-handed with Jason Koumas scoring the only goal of the game for West Brom in the first half.

21|10|03

	P	GD	PTS
2 West Brom	14	7	28
3 Sheffield Utd	14	9	27
4 Sunderland	14	9	27
5 Ipswich Town	15	7	26
6 West Ham Utd	13	8	25
7 Norwich City	14	5	25

Norwich City 2
Derby County 1
GOALS
Roberts (Pen)
Mulryne
ATTENDANCE
16,346

Against the odds City recorded a sixth home win of the campaign. On a wet night at Carrow Road City were reduced to ten men prior to the break as Kevin Harper saw red following a reckless challenge. Things went from bad to worse for City as the ten men then fell behind in the second half when Ian Taylor converted a penalty for the Rams. Yet again though the Canaries mounted a late comeback – Iwan Roberts converted a twice taken penalty before Philip Mulryne completed a remarkable turnaround with an injury-time winner.

Nigel Worthington and the Norwich bench show their delight at Philip Mulryne's late winner against Derby

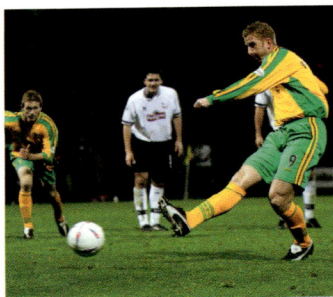

29

25|10|03

	P	GD	PTS
1 West Brom	15	10	31
2 Wigan Athletic	16	8	30
3 Norwich City	15	6	28
4 Sheffield Utd	15	8	27
5 Sunderland	15	8	27
6 West Ham Utd	15	8	27

Norwich City 1
Sunderland 0

GOALS
Francis
ATTENDANCE
16,427

After missing the last two matches through injury, Darren Huckerby returned to spearhead the City attack against fellow promotion hopefuls Sunderland. A closely contested affair was settled by Damien Francis' third goal of the season midway through the first half. The Wearsiders' cause was dealt a further blow when John Oster was dismissed for kicking out at City captain Adam Drury.

Sunderland's John Oster loses his cool and kicks out at Adam Drury

Darren Huckerby prepares to set off on another forward run

Damien Francis fires home the only goal of the game before being congratulated by his team-mates

01|11|03

Walsall 1
Norwich City 3

GOALS

Henderson

McVeigh

Crouch

ATTENDANCE

8,331

The Canaries' 3–1 away win at Walsall was arguably their best away performance of the 2003–04 campaign. Despite trailing 1–0 at the break, City played some great football and it was only a matter of time before their approach play was rewarded with goals. Ian Henderson drew City level soon after the re-start before further goals from Peter Crouch and Paul McVeigh wrapped up a 3–1 victory.

08|11|03

Norwich City 3
Millwall 1

GOALS
Henderson (2)
McVeigh
ATTENDANCE
16,423

City's fine home form continued with a 3–1 win over Millwall.

Paul McVeigh opened the scoring before Ian Henderson chipped in with a brace before the break. Millwall managed a second-half consolation goal but never threatened a major comeback.

Malky Mackay clears from Millwall dangerman Tim Cahill

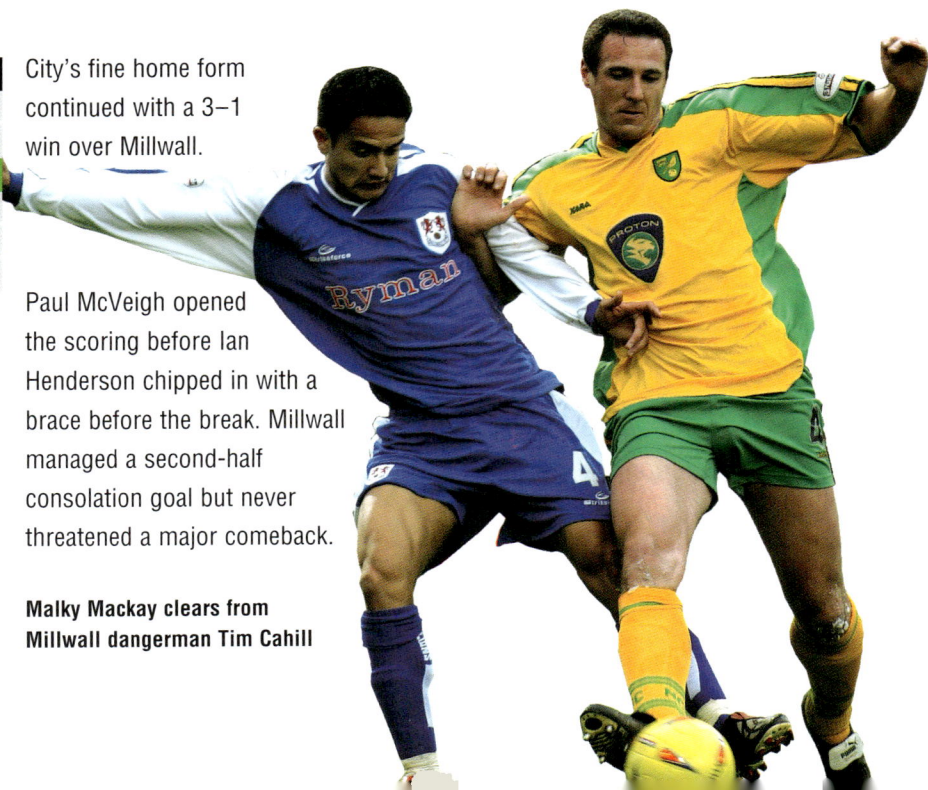

15|11|03

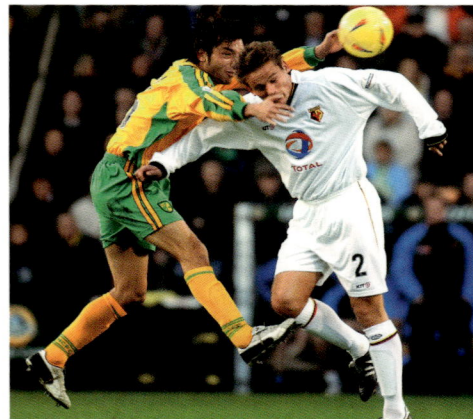

Norwich City 1
Watford 2

GOALS

Jarvis

ATTENDANCE

16,420

After winning their opening eight home league games the Canaries suffered a shock defeat against lowly Watford. The match offered the Canaries a chance to go to the top of the table but it turned into a missed opportunity on a frustrating afternoon for Nigel Worthington's side. One down at the break and with two strong penalty claims turned down – it was clear this was not to be City's day. Watford doubled their lead from the spot but were given a testing final few minutes after Ryan Jarvis reduced the arrears late-on. It was Jarvis' first goal for the Club and one that saw him take the mantle of being the Club's youngest goalscorer.

Ian Henderson goes close with a diving header

34

16|11|03

UEFA Cup reunion

The weekend of the Watford match saw the reunion of the Club's famous 1993–94 UEFA Cup team. A number of the Canaries' European heroes from ten years ago were introduced to the crowd at half-time during the Watford match with the majority of the squad then taking part in a European reunion function at Carrow Road on the Sunday evening.

Jerry Goss, Efan Ekoku, Colin Woodthorpe and Ian Butterworth recall the heady days of European football at Carrow Road

19|11|03

RETIREMENT

ALEX NOTMAN

Striker Alex Notman was sadly forced to retire from football at the age of 24. The former Scotland under-21 international had been battling for over a year with a long-term ankle injury.

22|11|03

		P	GD	PTS
1	West Brom	18	11	36
2	Norwich City	19	9	35
3	Wigan Athletic	19	12	34
4	Sheffield Utd	19	8	34
5	Sunderland	19	7	32
6	Ipswich Town	19	9	31

Preston N End 0
Norwich City 0

ATTENDANCE

14,775

The Canaries earned a valuable point from their long-haul north to Preston's Deepdale. In what was a somewhat dull game City showed true battling spirit and were grateful to some sharp stops from 'keeper Robert Green to keep the hosts at bay. The Canaries were up against a familiar face in David Healy, who spent a spell on loan at Carrow Road last season but Craig Fleming and Malky Mackay kept their former team-mate quiet.

Paul McVeigh tries his luck from a distance at Deepdale

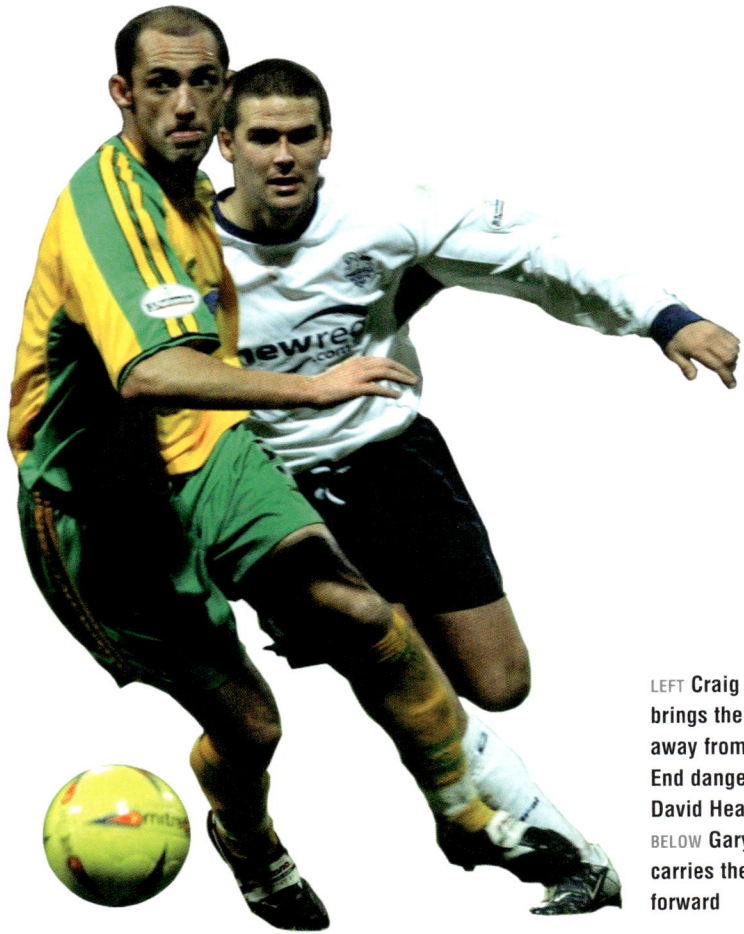

LEFT **Craig Fleming brings the ball away from North End danger man David Healy**
BELOW **Gary Holt carries the ball forward**

Iwan Roberts goes up for a header

25|11|03

	P	GD	PTS
1 West Brom	19	11	37
2 Norwich City	20	9	36
3 Wigan Athletic	19	12	34
4 Sheffield Utd	19	8	34
5 Sunderland	19	7	32
6 Cardiff City	19	14	31

Norwich City 1
Coventry City 1

GOALS
Henderson
ATTENDANCE
16,414

At a rain-soaked Carrow Road the Canaries were forced to share the points against an impressive Coventry side. City started well with Ian Henderson firing home his fourth goal of the season. Coventry forced an equaliser from the penalty spot early in the second half and when the Canaries were later reduced to ten men, following a second cautionable offence by Malky Mackay, all the chances fell to the visitors who may have felt unlucky not to have won the match.

ABOVE **Marc Edworthy slides in to block a Coventry shot**
ABOVE RIGHT **Gary Holt unleashes a shot despite the efforts of Julian Joachim**

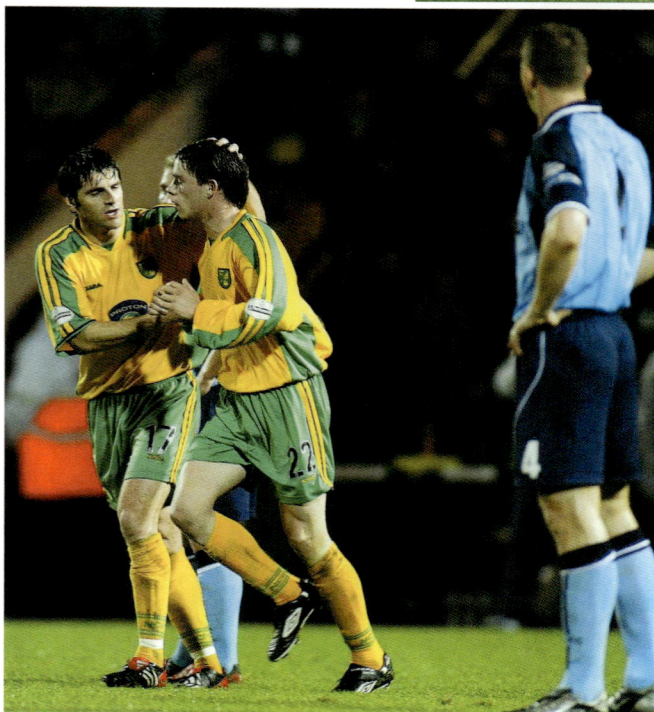

Ian Henderson is congratulated by Marc Edworthy

29|11|03

	P	GD	PTS
1 West Brom	20	14	40
2 Norwich City	21	10	39
3 Sheffield Utd	20	10	37
4 Ipswich Town	20	10	34
5 Wigan Athletic	20	8	34
6 Reading	21	4	34

Norwich City 1
Crewe Alexandra 0

GOALS
Huckerby
ATTENDANCE
16,367

After eight games without a goal Darren Huckerby curled home a first-half winner to get the Canaries back to winning ways against Crewe Alexandra at Carrow Road. Despite dominating the majority of the contest City were unable to add to their lead.

06|12|03

	P	GD	PTS
1 West Brom	21	14	41
2 Norwich City	22	10	40
3 Ipswich Town	22	11	38
4 Sheffield Utd	21	9	37
5 Reading	22	6	37
6 Wigan Athletic	22	6	35

Millwall 0
Norwich City 0

ATTENDANCE
9,850

The Canaries started the month of December with a quick re-match with Millwall. In a match that never really got going the Lions were unable to gain any revenge for their 3–1 defeat at Carrow Road the previous month. The game signalled the end of Peter Crouch's loan spell with Norwich and the dismissal of Millwall defender Kevin Muscat for a challenge on Darren Huckerby.

06|12|03

LEAVES
PETER CROUCH

Peter Crouch returns to Aston Villa after spending a successful three-month loan spell with the Canaries when he scored 4 goals in 15 appearances.

11|12|03

SIGNING
LEON McKENZIE

With Peter Crouch back at Villa Park and Darren Huckerby's return to Manchester City imminent, Nigel Worthington swoops for Peterborough United striker Leon McKenzie, the 25-year-old joined Norwich on a three-and-a-half-year contract.

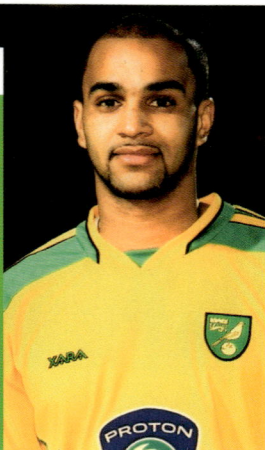

13|12|03

	P	GD	PTS
1 West Brom	23	15	45
2 Norwich City	23	13	43
3 Sheffield Utd	23	11	41
4 Ipswich Town	23	11	39
5 Wigan Athletic	23	7	38
6 West Ham Utd	23	11	37

Captain Adam Drury nicks the ball away from Cardiff's Richard Langley

Norwich City 4
Cardiff City 1

GOALS
Huckerby (2)
Roberts
Fleming
ATTENDANCE
16,428

In what was billed as Darren Huckerby's farewell match – the Carrow Road favourite bowed out in real style. From start to finish Huckerby terrorised an over-worked Cardiff defence, scoring twice and laying on countless chances for others in a 4–1 rout.

Darren Huckerby prepares to run at the Cardiff defence once again

17|12|03

SIGNING

MATHIAS SVENSSON

With Darren Huckerby back at Manchester City, boss Nigel Worthington strengthened his squad with the signing of Charlton's Swedish striker Mathias Svensson.

21|12|03

	P	GD	PTS
1 Norwich City	24	15	46
2 West Brom	24	14	45
3 Sheffield Utd	23	11	41
4 Wigan Athletic	24	8	41
5 Ipswich Town	24	9	39
6 West Ham Utd	24	11	38

Ipswich Town 0
Norwich City 2

GOALS

McKenzie (2)

ATTENDANCE

30,152

Norwich unleashed their new-look strike force of Leon McKenzie and Mathias Svensson on local rivals Ipswich Town for the first East Anglian derby of the season. McKenzie marked his debut with both goals to give City fans the perfect Christmas present and fire his new club to the top of the Nationwide First Division.

26|12|03

SIGNING
HUCKERBY

Majority Shareholders Delia Smith and Michael Wynn Jones give the Carrow Road faithful a wonderful late Christmas present as they unveil Darren Huckerby as a permanent Norwich City player ahead of the televised match with Nottingham Forest.

26|12|03

	P	GD	PTS
1 Norwich City	25	16	49
2 West Brom	25	14	46
3 Sheffield Utd	24	12	44
4 Ipswich Town	25	10	42
5 Sunderland	25	10	41
6 Wigan Athletic	25	7	41

Norwich City 1
Nottm Forest 0

GOALS

Svensson

ATTENDANCE

16,429

The Canaries made it a very merry Christmas as they extended their lead at the top of the table. After Leon McKenzie grabbed the headlines with his brace at Portman Road now it was the turn of Mathias Svensson to win a new army of fans as his first-half strike settled a tight game in City's favour.

LEFT **Marc Edworthy and Ian Henderson combine to thwart one-time Canary target Gareth Taylor**

43

28|12|03

	P	GD	PTS
1 Norwich City	26	20	52
2 West Brom	25	14	46
3 Sheffield Utd	25	12	45
4 Sunderland	26	12	44
5 Ipswich Town	26	8	42
6 Wigan Athletic	26	7	42

Derby County 0
Norwich City 4
GOALS
Fleming
Mackay
McVeigh
McKenzie (Pen)
ATTENDANCE
23,783

On the back of the excitement following the permanent arrival of Darren Huckerby, the league leaders finished 2003 in style by crushing George Burley's Derby County at Pride Park. Second-half goals from Malky Mackay, Craig Fleming, Paul McVeigh and a Leon McKenzie penalty saw City move 6 points clear of second placed West Bromwich Albion with an exciting 2004 on the agenda.

10|01|04

	P	GD	PTS
1 Norwich City	27	19	52
2 West Brom	27	16	50
3 Sheffield Utd	26	15	48
4 Sunderland	27	13	47
5 Preston North End	27	10	43
6 Ipswich Town	27	8	43

Norwich City 0
Bradford City 1
ATTENDANCE
16,360

Relegation-threatened Bradford City pulled off one of the shock results of the season in the First Division as they recorded a 1–0 victory at Carrow Road. On-loan Ipswich striker Alun Armstrong found the net on a day Norwich fans will want to forget.

Leon McKenzie attempts to get his point across to the match officials on a frustrating afternoon for the Canaries

LEFT **Paul McVeigh pushes forward for City**
ABOVE **Mark Rivers in aerial combat**

13|01|04
Manager of the Month award

With 13 points from 15 taken during December, Nigel Worthington landed his second Manager of the Month award of the season. Together with the rest of his backroom staff, Nigel collected the award at a Carrow Road presentation.

17|01|04

	P	GD	PTS
1 Norwich City	28	19	53
2 West Brom	28	16	51
3 Sheffield Utd	27	15	49
4 Sunderland	28	12	47
5 Ipswich Town	28	10	46
6 Wigan Athletic	28	9	46

Rotherham Utd 4
Norwich City 4

GOALS

Roberts

McKenzie

Huckerby (Pen)

Francis

ATTENDANCE

7,448

Keen to put the disappointment of the Bradford result behind them City travelled to Rotherham in a determined mood. The hosts had also suffered a recent upset, missing out on an FA Cup tie with Manchester United after bowing out in a replay against Third Division Northampton Town. In a real humdinger of a clash it was goals galore at Millmoor. Damien Francis was the hero with a late leveller for City in a game they could and should have won but could so easily have lost.

**All smiles –
Iwan celebrates
the winning goal**

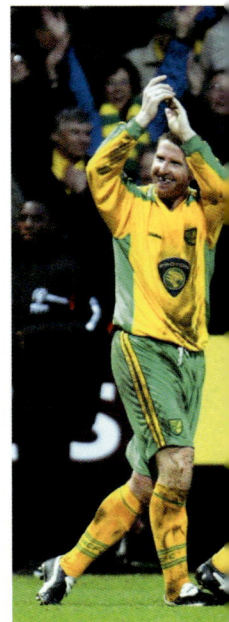

**Darren Huckerby
skips away from
his marker**

31|01|04

Norwich City 1
Sheffield Utd 0

GOALS
Roberts
ATTENDANCE
18,977

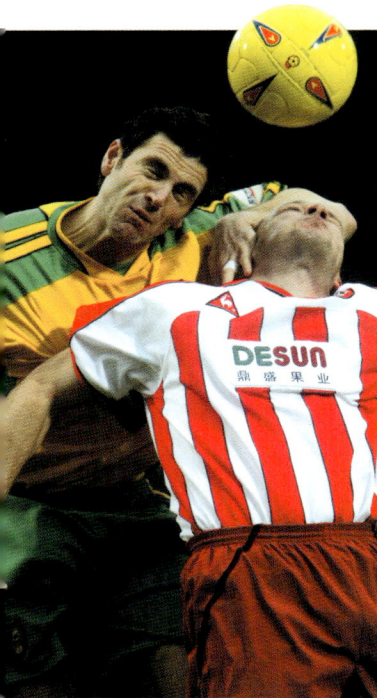

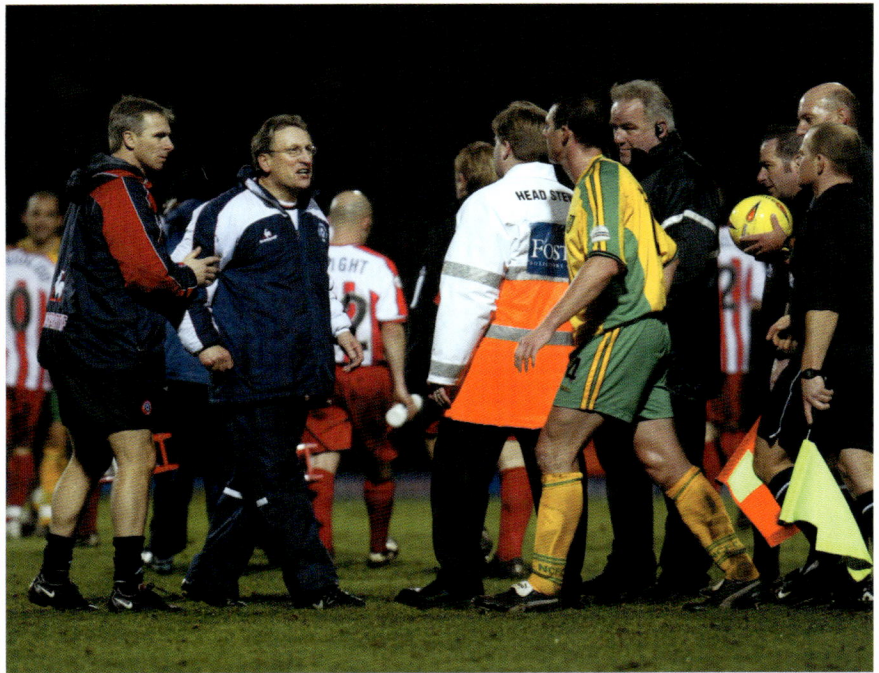

ABOVE **Marc Edworthy wins an important header**
TOP RIGHT **Jim Brennan puts United 'keeper Paddy Kenny under pressure**

Neil Warnock's Sheffield United arrived at Carrow Road for a real six-pointer. In true Sheffield United style it was a tough physical battle but the Canaries matched the men from Bramall Lane all the way and Iwan Roberts rifled home the game's only goal midway though the second half – certainly one of his most important goals for the Canaries.

Neil Warnock vents his fury on the officials as his side slip away from the promotion picture

07|02|04

	P	GD	PTS
1 Norwich City	30	21	59
2 West Brom	30	15	54
3 Wigan Athletic	30	11	50
4 Sheffield Utd	30	9	49
5 West Ham Utd	30	13	48
6 Sunderland	29	12	48

Wimbledon 0
Norwich City 1

GOALS
Huckerby
ATTENDANCE
7,368

On their first visit to the National Hockey Stadium in Milton Keynes, City record a 1–0 victory over Wimbledon. On a windy afternoon, a wonder-strike from Darren Huckerby settled the match in City's favour against a Dons team that was reduced to nine men by the final whistle.

14|02|04

	P	GD	PTS
1 Norwich City	31	23	62
2 West Brom	31	16	57
3 Wigan Athletic	31	13	
4 Ipswich Town	31	10	5
5 Sheffield Utd	30	9	49
6 West Ham Utd	30	13	48

Highfield Road has hardly been the happiest of hunting grounds for the Canaries but it all came right for City on Valentines Day.

Coventry City 0
Norwich City 2

GOALS
Holt
Brennan
ATTENDANCE
15,757

After surviving early pressure from the hosts, City took the lead through a rare Gary Holt strike. It took a good defensive display in the second half to preserve the slender lead but a cracking Jim Brennan strike sealed the points late-on.

Damien Francis
stretches to win this
midfield tussle

Marc Edworthy
slides in to
disposess Patrick
Suffo

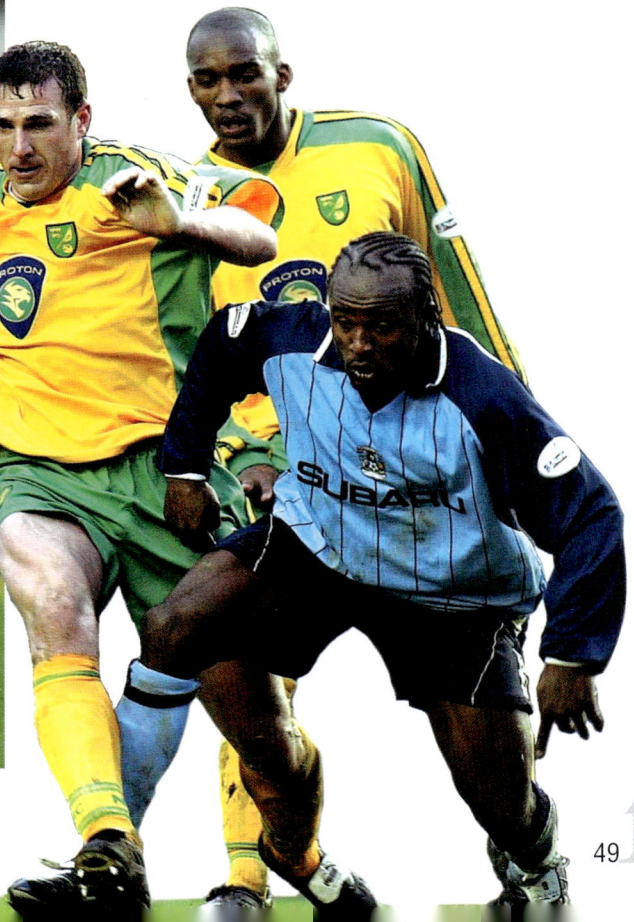

49

21|02|04

	P	GD	PTS
1 Norwich City	32	23	63
2 West Brom	32	17	60
3 Wigan Athletic	32	13	54
4 Ipswich Town	32	8	50
5 West Ham Utd	31	13	49
6 Sheffield Utd	31	8	49

BELOW Fans hold up green and yellow cards to celebrate the opening of the Jarrold Stand prior to City's match with West Ham United

FAR RIGHT Darren Huckerby torments the Hammers' defence

Norwich City 1
West Ham Utd 1

GOALS

Huckerby

ATTENDANCE

23,940

Prior to the eagerly-anticipated match with West Ham United, the new Jarrold Stand at Carrow Road was officially opened by former City boss and Hammers' favourite Ken Brown. Having recently celebrated his 70th birthday Ken was joined by a group of players with strong links to both clubs – John Bond, Graham Paddon and World Cup Winner Martin Peters. The game itself lived up to its big match billing with honours eventually shared after Darren Huckerby cancelled out Marlon Harewood's opener.

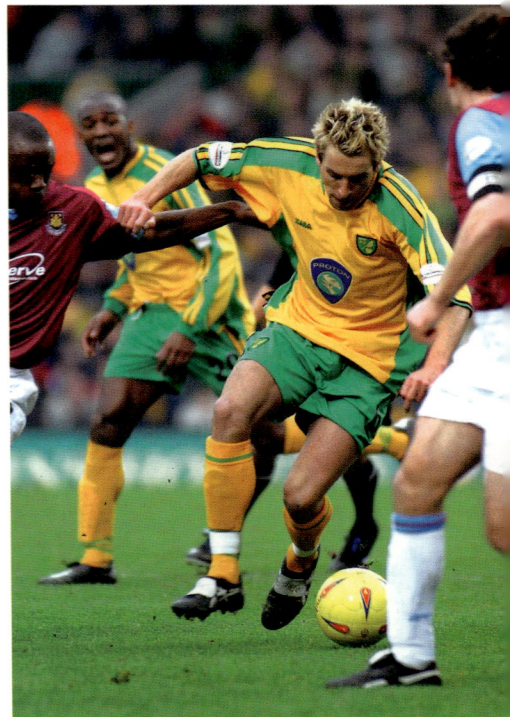

Happy Birthday Ken! Canary legend Bryan Gunn presents his former boss with a birthday cake

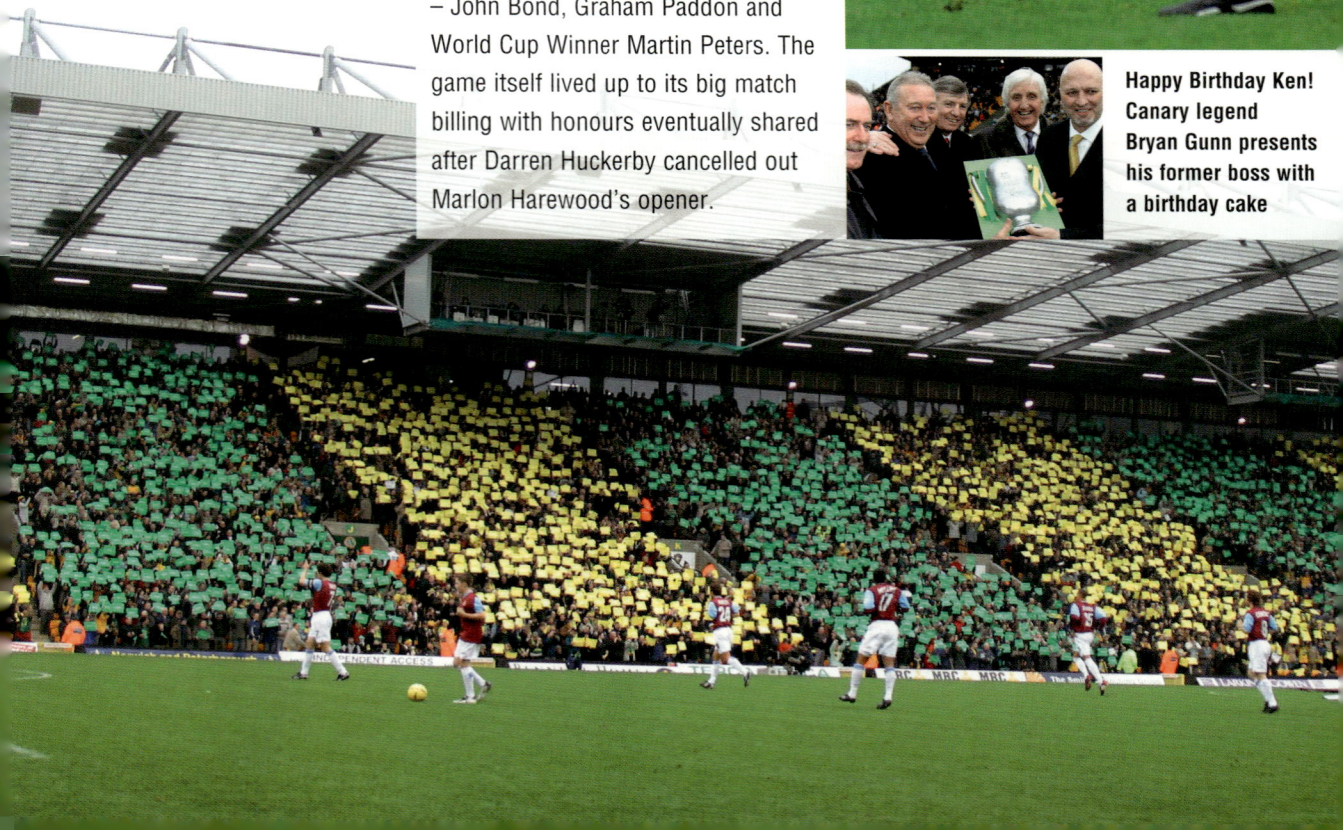

02|03|04

		P	GD	PTS
1	Norwich City	33	23	64
2	West Brom	34	16	61
3	Wigan Athletic	33	14	57
4	Sheffield Athletic	34	9	55
5	West Ham Utd	33	14	53
6	Ipswich Town	34	8	53

Norwich City 0
West Brom 0

ATTENDANCE
23,223

The top two went head-to-head in front of the Sky TV cameras and over 23,000 excited fans at Carrow Road. City had two strong penalty claims waved away by referee Brian Curson and despite dominating for large periods of the match the Canaries could not find a way past Russell Hoult in the Baggies' goal.

Battling for promotion – both Malky Mackay and Damien Francis give their all during a fully committed match with West Bromwich Albion

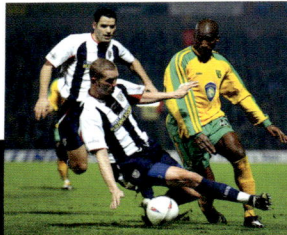

With the first East Anglian derby of the season going in the Canaries' favour, Town were gunning for revenge when they visited Carrow Road for a Sunday lunchtime showdown. The two arch-rivals were both keen for three points – City for their continued promotion assault and Town to keep their faint play-off hopes alive. Ipswich wasted a host of first-half openings and their inability to take their chances came back to haunt them as City ran riot in the second half. A brace from Malky Mackay and an own-goal from Georges Santos capped off a miserable day for the Blues who also had Drissa Diallo sent off.

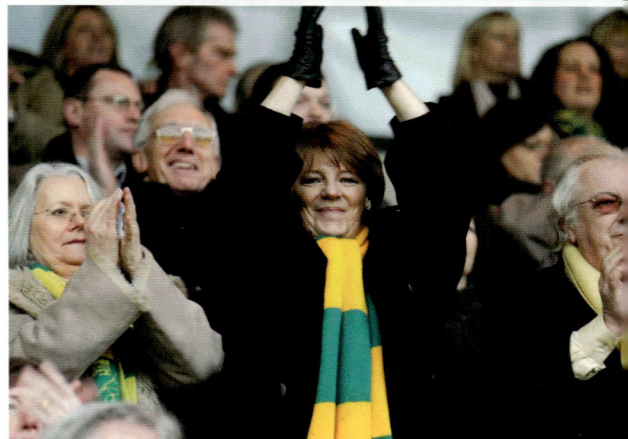

07|03|04

	P	GD	PTS
1 Norwich City	34	25	67
2 West Brom	35	19	64
3 Wigan Athletic	34	13	57
4 Sheffield Athletic	34	9	55
5 West Ham Utd	34	14	54
6 Millwall	34	8	53

Norwich City 3
Ipswich Town 1

GOALS
Mackay (2)
Santos (O.G.)
ATTENDANCE
23,942

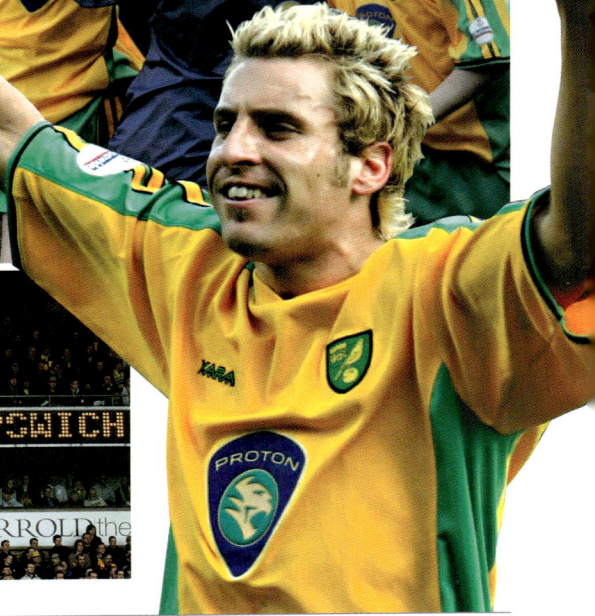

13|03|04

	P	GD	PTS
1 Norwich City	35	25	67
2 West Brom	36	19	67
3 Wigan Athletic	35	13	58
4 Sheffield Utd	35	9	58
5 West Ham Utd	36	14	57
6 Millwall	35	8	56

Cardiff City 2
Norwich City 1

GOALS
McKenzie
ATTENDANCE
16,317

The Canaries seven-match unbeaten run came to an end on a wet and windy afternoon in South Wales. A cross-cum-shot from Paul Parry eluded everyone in the area to give the hosts an early lead. The Bluebirds, clearly smarting from their 4–1 defeat at Carrow Road in December doubled their advantage before the break. City got back into the match early in the second half through Leon McKenzie but could not force an equaliser.

16|03|04

	P	GD	PTS
1 Norwich City	36	27	70
2 West Brom	37	21	70
3 Sheffield Utd	36	11	59
4 Wigan Athletic	36	12	58
5 West Ham Utd	36	17	57
6 Reading	37	-2	57

Norwich City 3
Gillingham 0

GOALS
Pouton (O.G.)
Mulryne
McVeigh

ATTENDANCE
23,198

18|03|04

ON LOAN

KEVIN COOPER

Ahead of the run-in to the end of the season, Nigel Worthington added Wolves' midfielder Kevin Cooper to his squad on a loan basis. The 29-year-old agreed to stay with City until the end of the season.

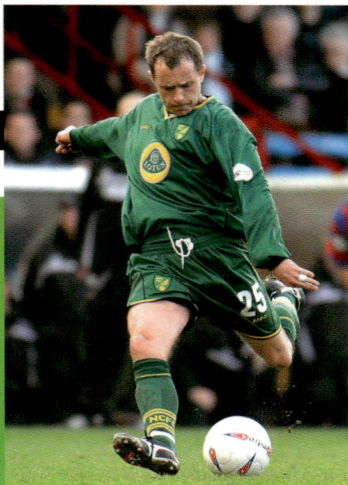

City bounced back well from the Cardiff defeat with a comfortable 3–0 home victory over Gillingham. After an edgy first half an own-goal from Alan Pouton set City on their way and further strikes from Philip Mulryne and Paul McVeigh wrapped up the win.

Paul McVeigh plays a ball up the line

20|03|04

	P	GD	PTS
1 Norwich City	37	26	70
2 West Brom	37	21	70
3 Sheffield Utd	37	13	62
4 Wigan Athletic	37	13	61
5 West Ham Utd	37	19	60
6 Sunderland	35	14	59

Crystal Palace 1
Norwich City 0
ATTENDANCE
23,798

Norwich were backed by almost 8,000 travelling fans for the trip to Crystal Palace's Selhurst Park. Sadly for the yellow and green army it proved to be a disappointing day out as City were defeated on their travels for only the fifth time this season. On an extremely windy day, the scrappiest of games was settled by a Wayne Routledge strike.

27|03|04

	P	GD	PTS
1 Norwich City	38	27	73
2 West Brom	38	23	73
3 Sunderland	37	16	65
4 West Ham Utd	39	17	63
5 Millwall	38	14	63
6 Sheffield Utd	39	12	63

Gary Holt battles with Carl Asaba

Norwich City 1
Stoke City 0

GOALS
Svensson
ATTENDANCE
23,565

It wasn't a happy return to Carrow Road for former Canaries Darel Russell and Ade Akinbiyi as Stoke returned home empty-handed. Mathias Svensson gave City a first-half lead with his second goal for the Club. After Darren Huckerby failed to convert a penalty, City had to survive some late Stoke pressure but thanks to a world-class double save from Robert Green they held on for all three points.

27|03|04

Robert Green named in England squad

After his heroics saved the day for his club, Canary 'keeper Robert Green was called into the England squad for the forthcoming friendly international with Sweden.

03|04|04

	P	GD	PTS
1 Norwich City	39	29	76
2 West Brom	38	23	73
3 Sunderland	37	16	65
4 West Ham Utd	40	15	63
5 Millwall	38	14	63
6 Sheffield Utd	40	11	63

Burnley 3 Norwich City 5

GOALS
Svensson (2)
Huckerby (2)
McKenzie

ATTENDANCE
12,417

Not for the first time this season were the Canaries involved in an eight-goal thriller on their travels. There was no sharing of the spoils this time though as braces from Mathias Svensson and Darren Huckerby coupled with a Leon McKenzie effort ensured City ran out 5–3 winners over Burnley at Turf Moor.

09|04|04

	P	GD	PTS
1 Norwich City	40	31	79
2 West Brom	39	24	76
3 Sunderland	39	20	71
4 Wigan Athletic	41	13	65
5 Millwall	39	14	64
6 West Ham Utd	40	15	63

With City still sitting pretty at the top of the table both their Easter fixtures were chosen for live television broadcasting. First up was a Good Friday match with fellow promotion hopefuls Wigan Athletic. A goal apiece after the break from Darren Huckerby and the in-form Mathias Svensson saw City take a massive step towards promotion with a 2–0 victory.

Norwich City 2
Wigan Athletic 0

GOALS

Svensson

Huckerby

ATTENDANCE

23,446

Mathias Svensson curls home the opening goal

Darren Huckerby celebrates his goal

58

Leon McKenzie looks to take
on the Wigan defence

12|04|04

	P	GD	PTS
1 Norwich City	41	32	82
2 West Brom	41	25	80
3 Sunderland	40	19	71
4 Ipswich Town	42	12	68
5 Sheffield Utd	42	9	66
6 Wigan Athletic	41	13	65

Reading 0
Norwich City 1

GOALS

Mulryne

ATTENDANCE

18,460

The Canaries completed the second leg of their Easter schedule with a tough looking trip to Reading. In an evenly contested match both sides created opportunities to open the scoring but failed to break the deadlock. With a goalless draw on the cards, Philip Mulryne was the first to react after the ball cannoned off referee Neale Barry. The Irish international sent a cracking effort flying home for an 87th minute winner – a strike that sent the 4,500 travelling fans wild.

17|04|04

	P	GD	PTS
1 Norwich City	42	37	85
2 West Brom	41	25	80
3 Sunderland	40	19	71
4 Ipswich Town	43	13	71
5 Wigan Athletic	43	16	69
6 West Ham Utd	43	16	67

Norwich City 5 Walsall 0

GOALS
Francis
McKenzie
Svensson (2)
Huckerby

ATTENDANCE
23,558

After collecting maximum points over the Easter period, City faced relegation-threatened Walsall in their next match at Carrow Road. Damien Francis got City off to a dream start with a goal in the opening minutes. Leon McKenzie then ended his Carrow Road hoodoo with his first goal on home soil. Further goals from Mathias Svensson (2) and Darren Huckerby sent all Canary fans young and old home happy, knowing their team had almost one foot in the Premiership.

Leon McKenzie celebrates his first goal for the Canaries at Carrow Road

61

21|04|04

Promotion

After Sunderland's defeat at home to West Bromwich Albion the Canaries knew that if Sunderland failed to win at Crystal Palace on Wednesday, April 21, then City would be promoted. A large crowd gathered at Carrow Road to watch a reserve match against Brentford and listen for news from Selhurst Park. A final score of Crystal Palace 3, Sunderland 0 signalled party night in Norwich.

Delia Smith,
Nigel Worthington and
Michael Wynn Jones
raise a glass
to promotion

We're back! City fans celebrate Premiership football with Delia Smith

24|04|04

	P	GD	PTS
1 Norwich City	43	38	88
2 West Brom	43	28	86
3 Sunderland	43	15	72
4 Ipswich Town	44	12	71
5 West Ham Utd	44	18	70
6 Wigan Athletic	44	16	70

Watford 1
Norwich City 2

GOALS

Francis

McKenzie

ATTENDANCE

19,290

RIGHT **Delia takes time to celebrate with the fans** BELOW **Leon McKenzie makes it two early in the second half**

ABOVE **City celebrate in front of their travelling army of fans**
RIGHT **Mathias Svensson wins a header**

With promotion achieved boss Nigel Worthington insisted his players must now go on and take the title. Once again City were backed in big numbers at Watford's Vicarage Road with City fans packing the away end and home sections too. The party atmosphere was made all the better by another away win as goals from Damien Francis and Leon McKenzie made amends for Watford's shock victory at Carrow Road earlier in the season.

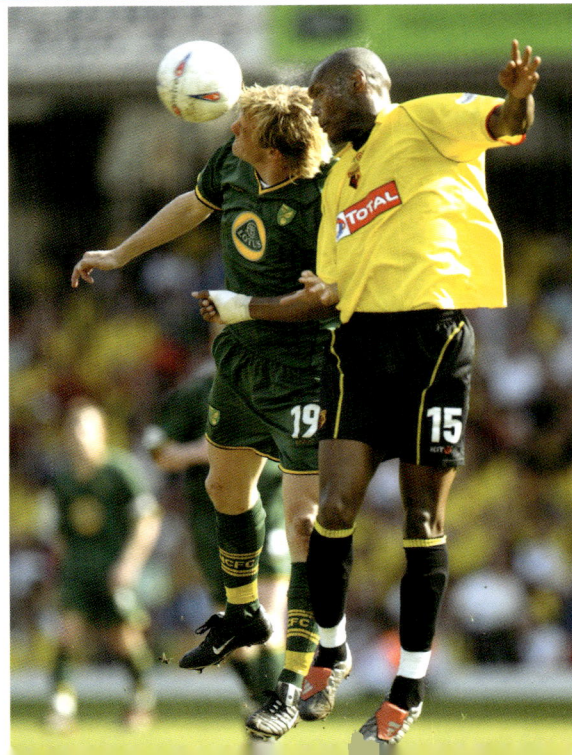

27|04|04

Player of the Year award

Darren Huckerby is voted the PFA fans' Player of the Year for Nationwide Division One.

01|05|04

	P	GD	PTS
1 Norwich City	44	39	91
2 West Brom	44	27	86
3 West Ham Utd	45	22	73
4 Sunderland	44	15	73
5 Crystal Palace	45	12	73
6 Ipswich Town	45	12	72

Norwich City 3 Preston N End 2

GOALS
McKenzie
Francis
Huckerby

ATTENDANCE
23,673

The final home game of the season saw mass celebrations at Carrow Road as the promoted Canaries took a giant step towards the First Division title. A 3–2 win coupled with West Brom's 1–0 defeat at Reading ensured that the Canaries could be crowned champions in three days time at Sunderland. The match was an emotional one for striker Iwan Roberts – the Carrow Road hero was playing his last home game for City after learning earlier in the week that his contract was not going to be renewed after seven years with the Canaries.

LEFT **Damien Francis is delighted with his wonder-strike**

01|05|04

	P	GD	PTS
1 Norwich City	44	39	91
2 West Brom	44	27	86
3 West Ham Utd	45	22	73
4 Sunderland	44	15	73
5 Crystal Palace	45	12	73
6 Ipswich Town	45	12	72

Norwich City 3
Preston N End 2

GOALS

McKenzie

Francis

Huckerby

ATTENDANCE

23,673

RIGHT **Iwan bids farewell to Carrow Road**

Team spirit – the squad celebrate in front of an adoring Barclay after the traditional lap of honour

01|05|04
Player of the Year award

Prior to kick-off ever-present defender Craig Fleming picked up the Barry Butler memorial trophy having been voted the Anglian Player of the Season by the fans.
In one of the closest run votes of recent seasons, Darren Huckerby was runner-up with 'keeper Robert Green third.

04|05|04

	P	GD	PTS
1 Norwich City	45	38	91
2 West Brom	45	24	86
3 Sunderland	45	16	76
4 West Ham Utd	45	22	73
5 Crystal Palace	45	12	73
6 Ipswich Town	45	12	72

Sunderland 1
Norwich City 0

ATTENDANCE
35,174

City set off on the long-haul north to Sunderland knowing that a point from their trip to the Stadium of Light or West Brom failing to win at Stoke would see City crowned Nationwide First Division champions. The visitors started brightly but were unable to turn their opportunities into goals. Despite falling behind to a Carl Robinson effort on the stroke of half-time, West Brom were well on their way to a 4–1 defeat at Stoke. Long before the final whistle the travelling fans were celebrating their team's return to the top-flight as champions!

LEFT **Celebration time in the City changing room after the Sunderland match**

07|05|04
New away kit

Top scorer Darren Huckerby models the Canaries' new look away kit for 2004–05. This shirt will be worn during the Premiership away matches at Tottenham Hotspur, Liverpool, Manchester City, Chelsea, Birmingham City, Aston Villa, and Fulham.

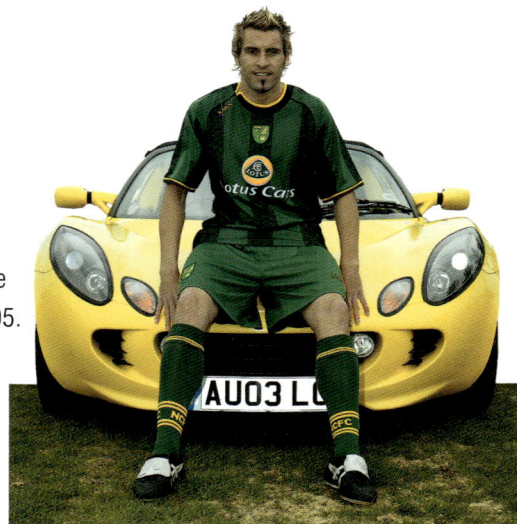

09|05|04

	P	GD	PTS
1 Norwich City	46	40	94
2 West Brom	46	22	86
3 Sunderland	46	17	79
4 West Ham Utd	46	22	74
5 Ipswich Town	46	12	73
6 Crystal Palace	46	11	73

Crewe Alexandra 1
Norwich City 3

GOALS
Fleming
Roberts (2)
ATTENDANCE
9,833

The final away match of the season was all about one man – Iwan Roberts. With 94 Canary goals to his credit the giant Welshman went into his final game for the Canaries wearing the captain's armband. In a fairytale finish to his Norwich career the crowd favourite netted a brace to finish his Carrow Road career on 96 goals.

Fans continue to party at Crewe's Gresty Road

The 'flying Flem' – Craig Fleming celebrates opening the scoring against Crewe

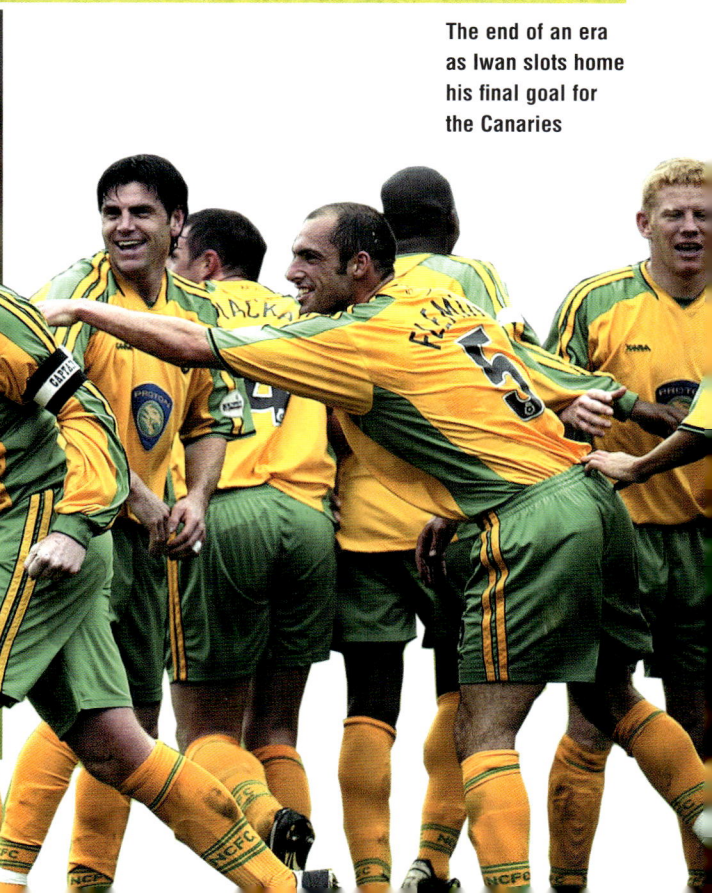

The end of an era
as Iwan slots home
his final goal for
the Canaries

10|05|04

Civic Reception

RIGHT **The champions' medals await their owners**

BELOW, FROM LEFT TO RIGHT

In safe hands – 'keeper Robert Green proudly holds the trophy; boss Nigel Worthington and his family take their turn with the famous trophy; mission accomplished for majority shareholders Delia Smith and Michael Wynn Jones; Marc Edworthy and his young family reflect on a great first season with the Canaries

Having landed the title after completing their Carrow Road fixtures, the Club were presented with the Football League trophy at a Civic Reception at City Hall in Norwich on Monday, May 10. The event brought the City to a standstill as over 50,000 fans decked in yellow and green turned out to salute the champions. After being presented with the trophy and their medals, Nigel Worthington and the Canary squad then enjoyed an open-topped bus ride through the city centre to some truly amazing sights. It really was an evening when the City of Norwich came out to party.

10|05|04

Civic Reception

The entire city
centre became a
sea of yellow and
green as fans
gathered to see
Adam Drury hold
aloft the First
Division trophy

10|05|04

Club Captain and Team Captain take their turns with the trophy to the delight of the fans

THE PRIDE OF EAST ANGLIA NORWICH CITY

10|05|04

Manager of the Month and Manager of the Year awards

Having guided the Canaries back to the Premiership as champions, Nigel Worthington received his third Manager of the Month award during the civic celebrations. He went on to also be named Division One Manager of the Year by his fellow managers.

Norwich City

Football Club